The Gift Within Me

The Gift Within Me

Karen Monterio-Moore

authorHOUSE®

AuthorHouse™
1663 Liberty Drive
Bloomington, IN 47403
www.authorhouse.com
Phone: 1-800-839-8640

Published by AuthorHouse   11/27/2012

ISBN: 978-1-4772-9121-4 (sc)
ISBN: 978-1-4772-9122-1 (e)

Library of Congress Control Number: 2012921964

Acknowledgement

I would like to say I am very blessed to be able to help and guide all the people that I do. My life and my experiences it is a road with bumps at times, but I would not trade it for the world. I thank all of my clients old and new for being such a big part of my life. Thank you my children for loving me and understanding my psychic gift. Thank you to all of the spirits that have been in and out of our home. God Bless you and Blessed Be.

"I ask that no negative energy or forces come to harm me or my family in any way for me writing this true life story of my life as a natural born psychic that has many unique skills with my gift. Blessed Be."

My story is about my life as a psychic. I was born with the greatest gift to see the past present and future. I have helped so many people throughout my life. When I was born, my mother said there was a veil over my head. She told me that when the doctor laid me across from her, I turned my head and she looked at me, and said she was shocked, my eyes where as black as coal. She said, at that moment she knew I was different.

As time went by and I got older, I started seeing things before they would happen. I would go and tell my mother and she would ask me how I knew these things. After a while, I began seeing people, which I now know were spirits. When you are a child, you do not understand what is happening. My mom could not help me, so she started telling me she did not want to hear what I had to say. When I told her things, I would get a spanking, so I learned to keep quiet and deal with what I was going through myself. It was very hard because I needed someone to talk too. Raised in a catholic family, things like this were not talked about. That is why I am writing this book about me, so all of you out there will know that you are not crazy, and this is real. We are the chosen ones.

Eventually, I started doing readings for people, and they loved me. They were so pleased with me, their faces where so surprised when I would tell them names of people and things that only they knew. As I began to understand just how special my gift was, it felt wonderful. I would help people with all kinds of things. I realized what I was seeing was called visions. I myself went to a woman who was gifted and she told me just what I have. She said," you were born with the gift to see the future and have the power to make things happen". She was so right, I have not only my psychic gift, I can will things to happen. Therefore, I started to help people, which then became clients of mine. I have had the same clients for many years. I have psychic gatherings with my clients and they bring their friends and family. At my gatherings, I put together herbs, oils, and chants for whatever their needs are as long as what they ask for is positive. I have been doing this for so many years. My gift can warn people about things that are coming their way. Whether it good or bad, happy or sad, I will stand by them no matter what. I believe I have this gift to help and guide people with their past, present and futures. I know there are children, teens, and adults that are like me all over this universe. I hope you all will take heed in my life experiences.

When I was about 12 my cousin and I were heading out to the carnival, we were getting ready to cross the street and I said, "no there is going to be an accident". Sure enough, right where we would have been standing a car crashed in that spot. My cousin looked at me and said, let's go home. That night, she asked me "how did you know there was going to be a car crash"? I told her that I just saw a car crashing there. I would tell her things that I would see she would look at me and just shake her head. She did not know what to say, I could tell she was scared, but she never stopped hanging out with me. I remember another time we were playing the Ouija board just asking questions then, all of a sudden, the board began to shake and the thing that our hands were on just flew off the board. We both were upset so we put the board away. The next day, I took the Ouija board out and burned it; I stood there and saw it turn black. Then

I put it in the trash outside. The garbage men picked the trash up the next morning, so as my day went on, I went outside and down the back stairs, and there it lay, like new, on the bottom landing. I knew that was not a good sign, so I never used a Ouija board again.

As time went by I married; I was very young when I married. I said to myself how can I tell my husband that he has married a psychic. Well, he started seeing things happening around our house like shades going up and down, chairs standing in the air; 6 chairs at that, salt and pepper shakers moving all around the dinner table. Therefore, I knew I had to tell him. One evening we were lying in bed and the shades started moving, I looked at him and said I have something to tell you; I was born with a special gift, he was just staring at me, I told him I can see things. He said, "What do you mean things? I said, I am a psychic. I explained to him there are spirits all around me. He replied," So that s what's been going on." he said he was trying to ignore what was happening. I asked him if he was scared, he said yes, but I love you and we made love that night. He was very understanding with what I explained to him.

As time went on we were blessed with four children. I was doing readings and feeling stronger and stronger with my psychic abilities. I was very interested in making things; like mixing herbs together. I would notice that I could make certain things happen like for example dry lavender made me feel very calm and peaceful. Therefore, I started to add a little myrrh to it for some protection and healing, then I added high john, for positive energy and all 3 herbs worked great together. I started to make different mixes of herbs for my clients and they worked for them, but before I gave my herbs to my clients, I would chant or say a prayer over them. Before I knew it, clients were asking me to bless their babies and their families'. People wanted to hug me after their readings, they would start crying and kissing my hands. I would say please don't kiss my hands, but they said I am so special that they just wanted to touch me, they knew I was a chosen one. I enjoy seeing the happiness and peace on their faces.

As I continued with my herbs, I started to work with crystals. Many years ago my daughter bought me a beautiful crystal. I always wear it along with my hematite and black onyx. By now I know, I am also a witch. All of these wonderful things I have been putting together for myself and clients are called spells. Wow! Psychic Witch, that's me. Blessed be mote it be. I am so proud of myself. Blessed with all these gifts I am helping so many people. Some of my clients consist of lawyers, state officials, police officers, doctors, pharmacists and many others from all walks of life.

Spirits who come to me and want me to tell one of their family members or friends a message for them appear during a reading.

Sometimes, when a spirit appears during a reading, I touch my clients hand, they can feel the coldness, and they can feel the presence of the spirit. The feeling that I get is something unbelievable. After my readings, I feel so peaceful to know that I helped with closure for that person.

A friend of mine called me one day in tears and told me here mom was not feeling well. Her mom and dad lived in Florida, we live in CT, and she asked me if her mom would be all right. As much as I wanted to say yes, I could not, I told her to prepare for the worst. She was taking a plane to Florida. I got the call her mom died. I felt so bad for her, we went to school together. We have known each other since 6th grade. A few days went by, I was going to bed, and I fell asleep. I woke up and I sat up looking at my doorway and standing there was my friend's mom who just died. A few days ago, she stood there in beautiful gown, it was purple, and she was showing me a necklace. It had different colors in it, it was big and she was holding it, then she was gone. Well, I was sweating, I woke my husband up and told him what I saw. He held me all night until the morning. I called my friend and told her what I saw and I told her what her mom was wearing. She said her sister was driving from Florida. They had her mom's body flown back to CT. She said her sister was bringing some dresses to pick from to put on her mom. She said I don't know what they look like so, she said she was going to call her sister and ask her what color where the dresses and she was also asking her about the necklace I saw on their mom. So we hung up the phone. She called me right back and said her sister started crying, she had the dress in the car and she also had the necklace with her. My friend said they were all in shock they did not know what they were going to bury their mom in but, because of me they knew what their mom wanted to be buried in, she had that purple dress and that necklace on when she was buried. I went to the funeral and they thanked me. She would come around me every now and then.

Another time, I was on the phone talking and all of a sudden, I saw someone hanging from my ceiling, of course it was a spirit. I had told my family what I saw; exactly what I saw already happened before anyone new. I received a phone call the next morning, one of my sons' girlfriends' cousin hung himself. I always make sure I tell my family or clients whenever I see something, that is called a vision, there are clients that have come to me and I would see or feel death around them, some want to know when or who, sometimes I can give a name or time.

One client had a family member in the hospital and everything I told them happened, even the time of death. She called me, and said, it was like reading a book; everything was exactly what I saw in my vision. The sprits are very tricky they move or drop things, they even touch you. Sometimes you can smell something very foul. That's also there way of letting you know there around. I always say if your evil be gone if you're not stay on. I have a house full of spirits. Some are waiting to cross over and some are here for protection, I call them the wonderers. Clients that come into my house say that they feel so peaceful and calm and that they don't want to leave, of course that makes me feel good. I believe that all the saints, gargoyles, eyes, energies, angels, crystals and my positive energy, along with my fairy's, herbs, oils and my cleansings, are a big part of what they are feeling. Most of the time I don't want to leave my house. It seems the minute I leave and go outside, I can feel the negativity. There are so many things going wrong in this world and times are so hard for everyone. Just walking down the street or by strangers, I can feel their sadness or pain and also there happiness. Many times when my family and I go out to eat, I just look around at the people in the restaurant and I find myself reading them. One of my kids or my husband will say "eat and stop reading everybody", they know me so well. I just smile and stop. Well let me go back to my psychic readings and my clients.

One of my clients came to me when she was very young. She thought she was in love, but I could see that the relationship she was in would not last. I kept seeing a shadow coming her way. A shadow is a male or female that will be with you like your soul mate. I told her that this was going to happen to her. I even described what he looked like. With the gift that I have, I block my family. People that are like me know what I am talking about. You don't want to see what is around your family. So some years went by and I was still telling her the same thing. Of course, she wanted to see this shadow. So, one day one of my sons saw her when she was leaving my house after a reading. He asked who she was; I said one of my clients. Therefore, he told my other son who was single at the time. My son asked me if she was single, at this time she was so, I said yes. He said I would like to meet her. I said really, so after a few days I called her and asked her, would you like to meet one of my sons ?He asked me to call you and ask you. So they met, whom I was describing all those years was my own son, but because I block my family, I would not let it through. They have given me a beautiful granddaughter. I have learned not to block my family all the time since this experience.

Onto the next client, One day I received a phone call from this women, she said I came highly recommended and she would like to have a reading. So we made an appointment to meet. She came in and sat down, she started crying. I looked at her and told her to save her tears and he is not worth it. I told her that she was wasting her time with her husband. I told her he was having an affair and that there was a baby on the way with the other women. Well she thought I was nuts. She said no way. "I have been married for 10 years, I know my husband and he would never do that to me. We have 2 small children and my dad just passed away and he was there by my side." I felt so bad to see her crying like that it just broke my heart. I told her I am sorry, but this is what I saw. I told her to go home and rest because all hell was going to break loose. So, that night she called me crying again. She had talked to an acquaintance and she told her what I had told her and the acquaintance confirmed it, her husband was having an affair, and the other woman was expecting her husband baby. I told her how sorry I was; she said she was going to confront him. She said he cried and said he was having an affair and they were expecting a baby. She kicked him out; she also found out that most of her so-called friends new about the affair. She grew up with these people, some kind of friends. She started coming to me a lot. She found a lawyer and got a divorce.

Her ex-husband ended up marrying the other women and getting a divorce. As for my client, she has moved on with my advice. I have helped her keep her house through my powers and herbs and chants. She also needed a new truck; I told her I would bring the truck her way. I made herbs and chants. She told me "if you can do this for me, I will treat you to whatever you want". Well she got her truck and I had a wonderful time with her treating me out. She kept the house and truck for a while. Then at another reading, I saw money problems coming her way. I told her beware of your house and sure enough, she got behind again with her payments. This time it was negative to keep this house. She was advised to sell, she did then she was ok and we lost contact for almost a year. I was having a gathering and I found her number and invited her. She came and told me she lost the truck. I was very happy to see her and she was happy to see me. She had no vehicle and was having it hard with 2 teens. You need a car, I said. I tried with my herbs and chants for her to, once again, have a vehicle come forth, and she has another vehicle. Now she has her own and doesn't have to borrow other people's cars, Blessed Be.

When my daughter was 9, I had a vision about her going into the hospital. I kept trying to block this vision, but it just kept showing me her in the hospital. Therefore, I sat my daughter down and told her what I was seeing.

I told her mommy keeps seeing you in the hospital, and I told her you will be fine, because I can see me combing your hair. So about a week later she came home from school, she said she was jumping rope at recess and her legs started to hurt real bad. Therefore, I took her to the doctors. Well, they took x-rays and said she had to be admitted right away. They had to do surgery on her hips. The bones had to have screws put in them, that's why she was having pain. My little 9-year-old baby girl looked at me and said you told me mom that I would be in the hospital. What a frightful feeling. I felt for her. I told her I love you and remember you will be fine. She had the surgery and everything went fine. She had a lot of pain, which broke my heart. She had and still has very long hair and I was sitting on her bed brushing her hair just as I saw in my vision. That was very hard for me but that is what happens when I do not block my family. When my daughter grew up she was expecting twins. Our family was so happy but as time was going by, I started getting that feeling that I get when something is coming my way. She was 6 months pregnant, I was talking to her and as I looked in her eyes I could see that something was wrong with the babies. So I told her I have to tell you something, your babies will be sick and they will go through a lot, but they will be fine. I wish with all my heart that I were wrong, so of course she was worried and started asking me a lot of questions. I just said prepare yourself. So the following month she went to the doctors the doctor told her they would half to take the babies out at 7 months and they were worried about their lungs. Because they were premature, she had developed toxemia, they put her in the hospital trying to keep the babies in as long as they could. She was so sick, I was standing beside her and she looked at me and said help me mom. I can't take this anymore. She was so swollen, so I called the doctors in and my daughter told them she wanted to sign a paper giving me the right to make all decisions for her and her babies when they were born and I did. I was right beside her when she had my grandsons. They handed the babies to me one at a time, she kissed them, and off they went. They were so small and they could not breathe on their own. One was sicker than the other was, it was very hard she was still sick, so I was asking all the questions and making decisions for the babies. When my daughter was well enough she took control of herself and her babies. One baby came home without the other twin, which was very hard for all of us. I knew everything was going to be alright. My husband and I would take turns with our daughter being with each baby. The baby that was in the hospital was having a hard time getting better the doctors were doing their best. My daughter asked me if I could make something for her baby that was still in the hospital, so I did. I chanted repeatedly and she put it on the babies little incubator. That baby started getting stronger his SATs went up and I told my daughter to remember the number 18. She saw that number and the baby was doing better and better. Before you knew it, he was home.

I want to talk about my angels ;We all have them, all we have to do is call them to us, there are so many. We have our own special angel that will help us with whatever we ask of them. The angels that I call on the most are Archangel Michael, for protection, Archangel Raphael, for health and stress release. Sometimes we take on a lot of negative energy from our family, clients and just picking up negativity from people we might pass in the store or in the street. I ask ST. Michael to cut the cords that are hanging on to me and he does. I also ask my guardian angel to sit with me and be with me every day to help me make decisions with my life and also how I guide my clients. I talk to the angels all the time and they show me how my life is supposed to be. I have many statues around my house such as fairies and blessed Mary. My saints will sometimes move or turn. When I am not feeling well, I ask my guardian angel to come and sit with me and to help me feel better. The angel's band together, they watch and wait to be called upon. Having so many spirits, around me all the time, it is also nice to have the angels near. I also like to write chants:

"Angles of mine, I hold so close knowing that you love me the most you spread your wings around me so tight that's what gets me through the night."

I remember when I was a teenager my mom gave me a picture of ST. Theresa, it was beautiful. My mom had this picture for years. I hung it in my bed room and I would pray to her all the time. My parents divorced when I was eight years old and that was a very sad time for me. Therefore, I would pray and sometimes cry. One day I was praying to St. Theresa; I was looking at her face and she started to cry with me. The tears were coming down her cheek she was crying. I believe because of my sadness. I also remember as a small child, I was about 6, my parents were still together, my mom put me to bed and said goodnight. I was lying in my bed with my cat Calago. There was a picture of Jesus above my bed and it would change pictures; that is how it was made. So I was lying down and all of a sudden my cat jumped and my hand was lifted up through my head and up to the picture of Jesus. The most beautiful breath of air coming from Jesus blew in my hand. I was so scared. Then my hand went back through my head. I remember looking at my hand to see if there was blood on it, because it just went through my head. I waited a few seconds, ran out of my room, and told my mom. She listened and she was surprised. She would never talk to me about that night. Years later, she said, "I know that happen to you". She just could not explain it to me. I believe that happen to me that night because I am a chosen one. There are people who will doubt my story and there will be people who will believe my story, all that is in this book I am writing, is the truth. This is my life and everything is real.

One day went to a priest and had a talk with him. I told him about my gift and he just listen. Years later, I went to the same church to light a candle and that same priest was there. He was very sick. He was in the church listening to confessions. Therefore, I decided to sit down with him and do a confession that day. It seemed that something was drawing me into that room. I felt like I had to do a confession with him (even though I do not believe in confessions). I walked into the room and sat down with him, I asked him for a prayer that would cover everything in one prayer. He said say the Serenity Prayer. I said to him "how are you feeling". He replied "Not well". He looked at me and asked me to pray for him. I told him, I will. He said "right now" and I said "here, right now", he said yes. So I started praying aloud and he put his head down, closed his eyes, and folded his hands together while I prayed. At that moment, I knew that he was aware of my gift. Our eyes met and he said " thank you". I felt so good inside when I left that room. Not long after that, he passed away. That is why I always tell my clients and my family "God always leads people to me or me to them". In this case, I feel I was supposed to be there, in that church, with that priest.

I would like to talk about another vision that I had about a family member. I saw this family member going to the hospital. I called her and asked her if she was all right, I told her I was very concerned. I told her about my vision she started crying, she said she was having very bad pains in her stomach and leg. I told her to go to the hospital. I told her she was pregnant but she said she had her tubes tied. I told her; please go to the hospital now. When she got there, they had to do emergency surgery. She was pregnant in her tube, she could have died. She thanked me for saving her life. Whenever we are together, she always tells me how she is so glad she listened to me that day.

Everyone asks, how do I know everything and how does it feel to have such a gift ?They always say they wish they had my gift. I tell them I feel so blessed to be able to help and guide everyone, but don't want to walk in my shoes. Trust me; they were made for me only.

To walk my shoes is not to be,

> For these shoes are made for me,
>
> Not too big, not too small,
>
> Just big enough to help you all).

Another client I want to tell you about is a woman that has been with me for year's. Her daughters and she have been my clients for 12 years. One day her daughters called me and said they were worried about their mother. She was not acting like herself, they felt that someone put a curse on her. So, they asked me if I would see her, I said of course. So she came to see me, I could not believe my eyes, she looked so different. She had an expression on her face that I never seen before. I told her to sit down. I ask her what was wrong. She just stared at me. I told her your daughters are very concerned about you. She did not answer me so I knew I had to cleanse her and take all of the negativity away from her. I started chanting and burning sage. I blessed her with holy water and I called the Archangel Michael and Archangel Raphael to come and protect both of us from this evil. I also put a protective shield over us, then all of a sudden I felt calm and she started saying` `Alleluia, Alleluia" and started turning in circles. I touched her hands and she called out my name and the evil was gone. She looked at me and said thank you. Her whole appearance had changed. She had her usual look on her face, she was no longer staring, she said she felt like something had control over her, until I intervened. She was very happy that she came to me and that her daughters called me. I was so pleased with the outcome of this cleansing. I have done so many cleansings on people and their homes and it is such a big part of my life to be able to use my powers to help others.

I want to tell everyone about one of my visions about one of my sons. One morning when I awoke I had my son on my mind. I think of my children all the time every day. I always put a protective shield over them but this morning was different. Something was wrong. I could feel it. As I said earlier, I try not to block my children anymore. so I started to see a vision of my son, he was calling out to me, so I send his guardian angle to him right away. Then I picked up the phone and called him, but there was no answer. I kept calling and calling and still, no answer. I just started chanting and calling for all the bands of angels to come down and protect him. I had to get ready to go and pick my mother up, we were going shopping that day, so I thought. So I tried calling one more time before I left my house. So I got to my mom's house she got in my car and I started to pull away. My phone rang, it was my daughter, she said my son was ok but someone walked up to his car and shot at him. He was able to put his car in reverse and get away by driving backwards out of his yard. The other person kept shooting at him, I was in shock. I could not move. All I did is scream as loud as I could. My mom looked at me. She was talking but I could not hear her. So I told her she had to stay at her house. We didn't even get out of her parking lot when I received the call. So she went back into her house. My daughter was still on the phone and started telling me what happened. Some man came up to my son and started shooting at him. He had time to call the police and he drove while the man was shooting "OMG". The police surrounded my sons car to protect him. My older son went to be with his brother. The man was calling the police saying he was going to kill the police that were chasing him. I just wanted to get to my son, but the police would not let me. I had to go back to my home and wait there with police all around my house, helicopters over my house, because the state police were in a car chase with this man. They were not letting me leave my house until they caught this man. My phone rang it was my older son, he said he was with his brother and he was fine. I wanted to talk to my younger son but I could not, finally the officer at the door said they caught the man. This whole thing was even on TV that night. I just wanted to hold my son and tell him I loved him. He came to me and said "mom, all I saw was your face, I could feel you and the angels all around me". I looked at him and said, "I had a bad feeling when

I woke up about you so I sent my shield and the angels to you ". In his car there is a shape of an angel were the bullet went through. The angels are always waiting to be called upon. I know my shield and the angels saved my son that day and his beliefs, blessed be. No matter what I do in my life, my children always come first. The pain in my heart, I will never forget, having this gift makes things so much harder when it comes to your family. You can sense what is coming their way and if my feeling is bad, it is so unbearable waiting for it to show itself. Sometimes I can give warnings or what I call a, beware. I thank god and the goddesses and all my energies for what I am able to do.

One day my mother and I were going to the casino. I had called her and told her I was on my way to pick her up. She said she would be waiting down stairs for me so I put my coat on and was getting ready to walk out the door. I am never late, I like to be on time. All of a sudden, I took my coat off and started cleaning my house. I was wiping down the tables and I started vacuuming. Then I just stopped. I said what am I doing, my mom is waiting for me. I looked at the clock a half hour went by, so I hurried an got in my car and left. When I got to my mom's she said what happen, your never late. I said I do not know, I was leaving and then all of a sudden I started cleaning. She was surprised. Well we started driving and we were just talking, as we got closer to the casino there was no one on the road, it really looked deserted. Then we saw the state police and they were telling us to detour. They said there was a catastrophe. There was so many fatalities. That half hour that I stayed and cleaned, saved my life and my mom's. We would have been on that highway. I always put a protective shield over my family and I and I know that we were protected that day. When we did get to the casino we were very saddened about all those people who lost their life's. It was on TV that night, we were blessed. We said a prayer for all of them.

I would like to tell too about a dear client of mine. I have none her for many years I met her in a store where I used to do readings. The first time she came to me she said I don't know you, she was not sure if she wanted a reading or not. The person that she was used to going to was not there anymore, so I said if you would like a reading, I would be happy to give you one. Then she said ok. Well at that that time she had a young daughter about 11 years old. She showed me a picture of her. Well I told her she is going to be hand full. I told her to watch her closely, there was peer pressure coming her way. She was very surprised. She said her daughter was very quiet and that she did not go out a lot. I said well this reading is called a beware. She said ok and left. Well a week went buy and she called me and asked me if I would be at the store again. I said no,

I also work out of my house. So she wanted to make an appointment. I gave her one and when she came, she said her daughter was acting different. She started answering her back and not listening to her. She wanted to go out with her friends and she was not old enough at this time. Well I told her I tried to warn you that this was coming your way she said I know. I told her I would say a chant to calm her daughter down she was very thankful. As time went by, she was coming to me a lot. I was telling her things that were going to happen. Her daughter was doing ok for a while then she started fighting with my client. I am talking about fists fighting, punches being thrown, police being called, both arrested, it was terrible. She asked me to please help her, so I put a spell together for her and told her to put some crystals in her daughters room and by doing this her daughter seemed to start getting along better with her mom. Another thing that I told her to put in her house was the dry lavender in a clear bowl, because that brings peace and calm into the home. That brought some time out for both of them for a while. At this time they seemed to be building a relationship. I have worked so hard to bring positive energy their way. My client has been coming to me for 12 years. She tells me I am her guardian angel and that she is so happy that she has me in her life.

Another client I have, used to come to me a lot. One day she ask me if her sister could come and see me. I said yes, she called and made an appointment. She came and right away I saw that an illness was around her. We were having the reading and she started crying. I asked her why was she crying. She said she didn't know. I told her that her husband was a good man and everything with them was good but I was concerned about her health. She did not want to hear it, I said ok I will chant for you and she left. I would say about a couple months went by and her sister called me and said her sister was in the hospital. I felt bad but I tried to tell her at the reading. She did not want to know and it turned out she was very sick. It did not look good. One day I was cooking in my kitchen and I turned and she was sitting in a wheelchair (but she was really at the hospital, this was a vision) she was sitting with her arm in a sling; I said what do you want? She just sat there and starred at me. So, I called her sister and told her what happen. She said she was leaving to go to the hospital and she said she would call me when she got there. When she got there, she said her sister was in a wheelchair, with her arm in a sling, just the way she was in my vision, in the kitchen. She told her sister that I said she was in my kitchen and her sister replied," I was there because I want her to help me". Of course, there was nothing I could do for her. I told her sister to prepare herself and her family. Soon after that, she passed away. In this situation I tried to give a, beware, to my client. I only advise. The final decision is up to them. However, when I say beware everyone always listens to me. Whether it be doing reading s, saying a chant, putting herbs together, shielding, sending them positive energy or using oils, the one thing for sure, I am right and all my family, clients and acquaintances agree. If I sound confident, I am. I have been helping and guiding people all my life. That is why I was born with this gift to do all these wonderful things.

I want to talk about some of the things that I do at my gatherings. This a time when I get my clients together and we all talk about different things. They get to know one another, I do short readings, and then we have coffee and deserts. It's different because there is a lot of people around, it's not just myself and one client. My favorite gathering is Samhain, also known as Halloween. All of us bake things like cake, cookies, pies, banana breads and so on. There are many lost souls roaming around at this time of the year, trying to cross over. So we bake sweets with our own hands and share with each other and we leave a little treat out for the spirits that might come our way. We also are celebrating the witch's New Year. We really enjoy ourselves. We then sit around and tell about something that has happened in that year that we do not want to happen again, because it caused sadness to us.

Then I tell everyone to write down all the negative things from the year down on parchment paper, which I give everyone along with sage. Then we burn the paper with the sage, because the sage cleanses away all the negativity. Then after it cools, everyone puts the remaining ashes in a plastic bag and throws it in the outside trash at their own houses.

I want to talk about something that many people experience, dying and coming back to life. I remember my father telling me when he was in the hospital ; he could see the doctors trying to bring him back to life. He said he heard them calling him. He saw them working on him, he said he did not want to come back. He saw a beautiful light and he saw his mom, dad, and friends that have already passed. He said he did not want to come back but he did. That happen to him a few times from what he told me. He has passed away since then, but before he died, I had to tell him something. Therefore, I called him one day and said, Dad there is something important that I need to tell you about something that happened to me when I was thirteen years old. I used to see your mothers sprit. She had died before I was born. I only saw pictures of her. The picture he had would always change. She was standing with a long coat on, then she would have the coat off. Her arms were by her side, and then folded. Therefore, I would turn the picture around or lay it down. When I would turn it around or pick it up and she was back to the original picture. My father replied "your grandma would never hurt you so don't be afraid of what you see her do". I was so surprised that this was happening, so I started calling out to her asking her to show herself. She would come and stand in my doorway. I was not very happy as a child, so I would ask her to take me with her. Then she would disappear, and I would call on her again and she would always appear. Then one night something different happen to me, I was crying and calling out for her. Then all of a sudden, my body was so heavy, I could not move, I could just open my eyes and I saw the most beautiful light with gates, angels, white clouds and a man. The man said it is not your time; you have so much to do. I have to call this man god. It was the most 'amazing thing that I ever saw. I know that I was in a different place, it was like I left my body while I was talking to him. All of a sudden, my body was getting lighter and I could move. From that day on, I never called my grandmother again. (As I am writing this experience, I am crying. I called my daughter and she came in my room and asked me why I was crying. I told her just give me a hug. She did and I feel better). Always remember, things happen in our lives for a reason. Mine is because of all the things I have done and still have to do. Having this experience was inconceivable.

Now I would like to tell everyone about the best place to visit for my family and I, Salem, MA the witch town. I have been bringing my children there since they were small and we always go at Halloween. All the festivities are wonderful and I always felt like I belong there. You can be you and there is so much to do at Halloween. I sometimes dress in my witch attire, but so does everyone else. The people are so friendly. Once I had my witch picture in the picture shop's window in the mall. My grandsons liked that. I went not too long ago with my son and one of my granddaughters for my birthday, so we stopped in one of the stores. I was looking for something, they thought they were out of it so the psychic witch came up to me and said she thought she had what I was looking for. She did and she handed it to me and she started to talk to me. She said she noticed I had a lot of black onyx on, she said sometimes that crystal can make you tired and have pain. I said to her I know that. She also said that I have a lot of power and I have good things coming my way, and that I still have a lot to do, I smiled at her. People were waiting for her but she came up to me. I said I know that. Then I said to her, people like us go through so much, our lives are very hard from others, she said yes. I know she lost her family in a fire and I felt very sadden for her. I thanked her for finding what I was looking for and my son, granddaughter and I walked out of the store. We stopped and were trying to decide, where we were going to eat. She then came out of the store and walked up to us. She looked at me and said, my son loves me very much. Then she turned to my son and said, your mother is very powerful with her gift and your daughter is just like your mother. She then turned to me and said your teaching your granddaughter well. I told her yes I am and I already told my son about his daughter's gift like mine when she was born. Then she said to my son let your mom teach her, she will learn well. I said thank you than she called me to come closer to her. She pulled out a silver box and she opened it, there were a women and a beautiful baby. She said that was her grandchild. I asked her if she was going to teach her grandchild, as I am going to teach mine. She replied, of course. Then we sent each other good positive blessings and said blessed be. We then walked away. We could feel our positive energy and we both knew we were powerful and Real. It was a very enlightening experience. When you are a gifted person, you know when another person is like you. That is a good thing. That is why it is so important that everyone who reads my book understand that I am trying to make you aware, of the importance of listening to our children. When they are small pay attention to what they say to you. For example, my grandchildren are gifted. One of my sons called me one day and said my granddaughter was crying, she told him she was seeing people in the house. I told him to tell her to say be gone. She was 2 years old. She does not know she is seeing spirits. He told her to say what I said, but she kept crying. So the next day she came over my house, I asked her what did you see? She said lots of people in her house. I explained those were spirits and she can see what no one else could. I told her that I could see the spirits when I was little like her. I do not want her to be afraid. So, I told her to say be gone, when you see the people. She says be gone and she does not cry anymore. I am glad that I can teach her what her gift is about. Her gift is like mine. She just turned 3 and I am looking forward to her using her abilities with me and her little cousins. My other grandchildren have gifts as well. My other 2-year-old granddaughter names the spirits she sees she plays with them. I told her no, we do not play with the people, we say be gone. She laughs, but I told my son watch her. Sometimes we have to protect the children. They are innocent and open to all kinds of spirits trying to cross over or trying to take over their bodies. I know, I been through it, that is why I am watching them and explaining whatever they ask or see. My other grandchildren are twins. I call them the watchers. They have the gift to see what is coming over the family. They are 12 years old, one of them we talk through telepathy; He thinks that is so cool. The other one never liked seeing people but he is still very powerful and we talk a lot about his gift. There is another grandson he is 2 years old. When he came home from the hospital he was laying in my room, I was talking to him. (you know grandma talk) He was looking at me and I said look at the picture of St. Anthony, he turned his little head and looked right at St. Anthony. Then I said look at St. Theresa, he looked at her picture. I was so happy he was only days old. My daughter told me at night when he slept, a red light would be over his face; he would glow. She would call me in the room and I would see this myself. I would say a chant and it would disappear. All things are real and parents should know what to look for. So pay attention to your babies'.

I want to talk about some more of my clients. This is another example of my gift. I had a reading with this client one day; I have known her for many years. Her father was also my client. She came to me first and what I told her happened so fast. I told her I saw her mother having stomach problems and I saw a lot of blood on the floor; it was a very negative reading. I felt bad but I say what I see. Well she left and a few weeks went by, then I got the call. Everything started happening but it was her father it was happening too, not the mother. Sometimes when people are very close, their energy can connect and in this case, that is what happened. She was very upset and worried. I told her, you try to be strong and that I was here for her and her family. Then one day her father called me and wanted a reading. I told him that it did not look to positive, which was very hard for me to tell him. Unfortunately he passed, he was a wonderful man and his family and I are very close, blessed be.

The next client I want to talk about I have known for many years, our families are very close. When they decided they wanted to come in for a reading, I was happy. I was over there house and as we were talking, I had a vision of a fire around them. Therefore, I told them about my vision and they just looked at me strangely. They did not seem to grasp what I was saying to them. Not too long after that day; there house caught on fire. I felt very bad for them, they called me and said I was right, I thank God and the Goddess that no one was hurt. With this same family, one day the woman and I were having a reading and she was asking about her marriage. I saw right away that a divorce was coming her way. Her husband and she were married for many years. Therefore, she said no way but I told her this surely was going to show itself, and it did. They divorced; I was very saddened to hear of the news even though I had seen it in the reading. Just because I see, what is coming everyone's way does not make me happy, I feel for my clients.

What I see with my eyes
Always helps me realize
All the things that I say and do
Are always visions from me to you.
Blessed Be

I would like to talk about some more of my clients. This client is related to me, we are very close we were babies together. We have pictures of us when we were very young and we have always been in touch. We almost talk every day. When she was going to get married, she was very happy. I on the other hand had that feeling that something was not right. I tried to tell her. I thought she should wait a little longer but she said she wanted to get married to this person. So she did and years went by, they had children, they bought a house, she worked hard and seemed like everything was good. Then we were talking one day and she was very unhappy and crying she said her husband was treating her very mean and she didn't know what was going on. I did, I told her I would come down and see her. When I got there she was a wreck, I told her she is a good person and she has to except what is happening; there was someone else in his life. I could see it when I looked in her eyes. I just held her and we cried together. I told her it would show itself. When anyone is doing wrong, it will always show itself. Therefore, some time went by and she called me and said she found out there was another women. She was very hurt, but she knew what she had to do for her and her children. She divorced him. I tried to tell her from the beginning that I saw so much negativity around him. Now I was there for her to try to help her move on. I would have her and the kids come over my house, and we would cook together her kids and my children got along great. Then one day when she was over, she asked me for a reading. I said ok, the first thing I saw was a shadow. A shadow is a person coming your way. I told her he would be her soul mate and he would love her like no other man. She said no way. I remember, she started laughing and I said she would marry him, and that his name stared with an S. I could not pronounce it because he was from another country. She looked at me and said, "If that is what you see, then at our wedding I want you to be my maid of honor." Well, I was the maid of honor, his name started with an S and he is from another country. The wedding was beautiful, they are very much in love, and they have been married for many years.

Through the eyes of the crystals

I am really into my work with crystals. They are so amazing when you walk by and the crystals call out to you, they can be used for so many different things. For protection, healing, to help with pain, stress relief, jobs, making changes in your life, love interest, and absorbing negativity. Amethyst crystal is very powerful. It enhances your psychic abilities. It also has been known to be a stone of royalty; it is utilized in crowns, scepters and the rings of bishops. It is said that the name comes from a Greek word "not drunken". It is also an ideal stone for enchantment; I myself have clusters of amethyst crystal in my home and my meditation room. I also keep some in my car. Placing an amethyst stone in one's room can help keep your healing space clear. (Of course, it can be in a room you are more comfortable in.) Some of the crystals that I use are the following:

* Malachite is for health and helps in healing. Hematite absorbs negativity, keeps negativity away from you. *Black onyx is used for protection but too much can make you feel tired, stressed and run down if too much is worn.

*Turquoise, in the Native American culture, is for protection. *Rose quartz is for love and relationships. Jade is for prosperity and is popular in the Asian culture. *Citrine is used to open doors that will increase clarity of things that you are thinking. It also has a powerful frequency that permits clearing and strengthens the manifestation of one will. I feel it is very positive for people born with this as a birthstone to wear it. *Blue sapphire it is an enhancer of insight. It can also stimulate ones psychic abilities.

I make sure that my family has their crystals' in their homes. I let them pick out the crystal that calls out to them and they always pick the ones that I want them to; but they do not know it at that time they are deciding. My small grandchildren are between 2 and 3 years old and they do the same thing. When they pick their crystal, I put them in a pretty bag and their parents put it in their rooms.

I would like to get back to my clients. One client holds a very important position in society; she has been coming to me for many years. Just recently, her health took a turn for the worst, but she came through. She asked me if everything was over and if she was in the clear as far as her health. I answered no. I told her that I see her going back to the hospital. She has gone back once so far. Then she called me and she was in the hospital again. These were short stays, but I told her in my vision she would be admitted to the hospital again. Everything I have told her has showed itself and she tells me I am always right. I told her do not' worry I will be here for you. Unfortunately, she has a lot to go thru, it's very hard for me to see all these negative things coming her way. She had to go back to the doctors like I told her she would. I am so sad about what I see coming her way.

I want to talk about myself a little more. I can remember when I was in grammar school my friends and I would walk to get on a city bus to bring us home. We would be laughing and talking about all kinds of things. Then all of a sudden I started noticing when I would look at some of the people that were walking or just standing, they had different faces under their skin. So I do believe there are other beings on this earth. No one else was seeing what I saw. They were looking at the same people that I was looking at and they never changed their expression. The thing is, I would start starring at them, and their faces would start changing right in front of me. I could see right thru them. While I was seeing this happen right before my eyes, I was wondering how long this has been going on, there are other people on this earth besides us. They can look human and in a blink of an eye, they turn into someone or something else. I feel with this gift that I was born with is the reason why I can see these changes. I know that there are other people in this universe that have the same gift that I do and can most likely see what I did. I hope that my book will encourage them to contact me.

I want to go back to one of my clients that I have already talked about in the middle of my book. She came for a reading a few weeks ago and I told her that her father's energy was not good. I told her to prepare herself. Well she called me and said I was right. He got very sick and he passed away. I went to her house to pay my respect she thanked me and said it was much easier for her because I told her it was coming soon. I try and prepare my clients with whatever it might be. I am there for them. (Blessings to her and her family). My client's father showed himself to me and he wanted me to tell his family that he is at peace with his wife.

When someone passes over and they want their family to know something the spirit comes to me and tells me what to say. Some spirits are stuck here and they sometimes can't cross over, for instance if it wasn't there time like an accident or suicide or murder, they are what I call the wondering souls. In those cases I will ask the family to come over and talk to me about doing something to help the sprit to cross over. The spirit's will show themselves to me while the family members are present and at that time we will make a decision. It is very hard in these situations, some families do not want to let go and they tell me they want their loved one to stay near; even though they cannot see them. Knowing that they are near comforts them. I tell them that they need to let go and they need to let their loved one know its ok to move on. Sometimes the families agree and sometimes they do not. This can be difficult when families will not let go. It is very understandable, but the spirit sometimes need's to hear their family tell them to move on or on some occasions the spirit wants to be forgiven or want's revenge. I have had experience with both kinds of sprits. It is not easy either way, but I confront what shows itself to me.

I hope people out there take heed in what I am saying, if you do not know what you are doing please do not dabble. It can be very dangerous. You can open up something that you are unable to handle. Sometimes people like to try things like spells or bringing sprits forth, and they haven't a clue of what they are doing. They can bring evil their way by doing spells the wrong way and this can bring a lot of havoc into their lives' and their loved ones. So beware, contact someone like me that is experienced.

I want to talk about another client of mine she was a very good friend to one of my sons she was going to college with my son. She told my son that she wanted to have a reading with me, so one day she called me and made an appointment. I saw so many things from her past as a child. She had been molested by a family member and blocked it from her mind all these years, until she came to me. I felt bad having to show her the past, but she started remembering and she cried a lot. She said she always knew something happened to her as a child, but she could not remember. As time went on, she started coming to my psychic gatherings and coming for readings. Then her grandmother, aunt and other family members were coming for readings all the time. They're wonderful people. One day my son called me and he was crying he said someone told him that his friend died he asked me to call her aunt and see if it was true, so I did and the aunt said yes she died the night before which was her birthday. I was so sadden. I tried to tell her to be careful something negative was coming her way. Her grandmother called me up and said she wanted me to come to her house, and I went right away. When I got there my son was there with the grandmother and when I saw her she and I just held on to each other. We were both crying she said the police killed her granddaughter. She asked me to see if I could feel what happen. I felt something very wrong. I could see her granddaughter on the ground and someone else with her. The police said it was a traffic stop and when she got out of the car, she collapsed. That is not what I saw in my vision. I saw her bullied by someone. The news people where at the door and the grandmother wanted me to go out with her to talk with them. I said no, let my son go with you and he did. It was on TV; that night with her, my son and other family members. She hired a lawyer because something was not right. The lawyer asked me to go to a vigil. They had found the other person that was in my vision. The lawyer wanted me to talk to him. I remember walking up to him and telling him what I saw, and he was saying yes, to what I was saying. What a needless death, she was a beautiful person, we miss her dearly; as for grandma, she sued the town and I heard she helped her family with what she got, Blessed Be.

The client I am going to tell you about has been my client for many years her family members are also my clients. They are wonderful people. One day she came to me for a reading. She was seeing this person for a while they started living together. I was very uncomfortable with this but she really loved this person. She asked me what I thought about him. I told her the energy was not good and to be careful, but she was following her heart. She did not want to hear it; she said he was giving her a ring. That didn't change my mind. I told her that he wasn't' the one for her and I left it up to her. Then one day she called me and said that her boyfriend's cousin moved in with them and she said she was not happy. She felt that something was not right. I tried to tell her to beware. Well, what happen was her boyfriend told her he was giving his cousin a ring too. She was very hurt and surprised. I was not; he gave two women an engagement ring. She said I should have listened to you.

I have told so much about some of my client's and some things about myself. There is something else that I want to share with everyone, it happen a short time ago. A client and I were talking on the phone. We wanted to go out for a ride. It was a beautiful day so we decided to get on the highway and drive. We were talking while she was driving all of a sudden butterflies and dragon flies stared hitting my window on the highway. I said to my client; look at what is hitting my window. She was surprised we could not understand where they were coming from. Therefore, she turned off the highway, and we came to a little town called Chester. We never heard of this place so we decided to stop and look around. We could see many shops. Before we got out of her car, I said to her I wonder what all those butter flies and dragonflies were about. Then I said I am thinking of honey she laughed and said honey. So we got out of the car and started walking. The first store we went into the woman was so friendly she asked us where were we from, I guess it is a small town. We told her and she said welcome to our town. She had beautiful Italian china sets. She said everything was made in Italy. We told her what happen on the highway and she said there is a lot of butterflies and dragonflies here, while she was talking, I felt a presence and I told her. She said those must be our fairies. Today there are a lot of them about, she said you must think I am crazy. I said no I can feel a lot of them present. I told her I am a psychic. I do not think you are crazy at all. She said that is wonderful. I gave her one of my business cards. She said she hoped to see me again. She told us to make sure and go to the fairy lady's store. We left and went to another store; it was a small museum with lots of art. So I told her I am a psychic and I keep feeling a very strong presence; she said it could be the Indian who founded this town many years she asked if it was a good presence or bad. She asked is there any evil in here. I said no I do not feel any evil, but there is something in here. I told her I was writing a book, she said when it's done let us know. She told us to sign a book, so we both signed the book and put our name and the date we were there. We left and went to another store. When I walked in I could not believe what I was seeing. There were butterflies and dragonflies all over the place, on napkins, pretty boxes, toys and more. I said to my client, it was meant for us to come here today. The butterflies and dragonflies wanted me here. I keep seeing honey in my mind. My client said what do think is going on, something wanted me here and I am going to find out what. So I wanted to see the fairy woman. So we found her, we walked in the store and I told her my name and that I am a psychic. I said I have all little fairies all over me and I am giving them to you and I told the fairies to leave me and stay with her. She was so happy. She welcomed us with open arms. We talked about a lot of things. She showed us fairy wings she made herself. She even showed me a tattoo on her back in memory of her mom. There where fairy houses that she made herself for the fairies to go into, it was wonderful. My client bought me a pair of fairy earrings and some purple fairy wings. What a nice place. The people were great. I gave her my business card and she gave me hers. I told her to take care of those fairies, and then we left the store. There was one more store we wanted to go in, so we went to it; what beautiful jewelry. They were all from estates. The women came up to us; she was very nice. We talked about how long she lived there. She told us she bought a barn, she was so happy living there. I would be too; as we looked around I said I do not buy used jewelry because I can feel the people that wore the jewelry. She said she understood. All of a sudden, I looked in a corner window I could not believe my eyes, so I said to my client go and pick that jar up and she did. She looked at me and said it's the honey you been seeing, the women said I brought that in today, she said I don't know why I did, my client just stood there in shock. So I explained to the woman about the butterflies, dragonflies, fairies, and honey. For some reason we were drawn to that town. We plan on going back. I have always collected fairies, I now have many butterflies, and dragon flies in my yard. It was a wonderful experience and I believe my fairies took me to that town that day and I am so glad they did they are all around my house flying around.

Printed in the United States
By Bookmasters